WITH **STILL SMALL VOICES** THEY SPEAK

February 14, 2002

This book is dedicated to the late Dr. Charles H. Wharton,
author of *The Natural Environments of Georgia*, 1978

WITH **STILL SMALL VOICES** THEY SPEAK

A journey into the heart of Georgia's last wild places

Ann Foskey *poetry & prose*

Marc Del Santro *photography*

Legacy Communications Armuchee, Georgia

Photographs copyright © Marc Del Santro
Text copyright © Ann Foskey
Photograph of Dr. Wharton © Ann Foskey

Contact Ann or Marc at nature@stillsmallvoices.org
or visit www.stillsmallvoices.org

Design and composition by Jeana Aquadro

Library of Congress Control Number 2006937479

ISBN 1-880816-24-5

Legacy Communications, Inc.
P.O. Box 585
Armuchee, Georgia 30105-0585
www.georgiabackroads.com

Printed in Savannah, Georgia

The paper in this publication meets the minimum requirements of the American National Standard for Information Sciences — Permanence of Paper for Printed Library Materials ANSI Z39.48-1992.

CONTENTS

PREFACE

Nature speaks to us in a thousand different ways — through our senses, through our bodies, and in our minds and hearts. Nature infuses our imagination, informs our language, and appears in our dreams. It populates our metaphors, our morality, and our myths. In the most basic of ways, nature gives us our breath, water, food, and shelter. We are a part of nature and nature is a part of us.

We all have an experience of this. Whether it is in the way our spirits lift when the sun comes out after many days of rain, when we catch the scent of wood-smoke in the autumn air, or when we hear the haunting cry of cranes in flight, we are moved and changed, uplifted and healed by nature.

Yes, we are humbled by nature's great power, by her winds, her waves, and other great forces. We know we are not in control; we are participants. And whether we realize it or not, we are stewards.

It is humbling to know that the exquisite expressions of life on Earth have been entrusted to our care. These beautiful and fragile creations, including all the wild places of Georgia presented in this book, are at the mercy of our behavior toward them.

The Still Small Voices project is a unique blend of art and science designed to promote the values of Georgia's natural communities. In a personal sense, it is an expedition into unknown territory, an exercise in listening with all the senses and in being present. We set out to discover what each of Georgia's natural environments is saying and to share what we heard with you.

Georgia's natural environments are not remote; they are just outside your door. We hope this book inspires you to explore more deeply your relationship with nature and to see what expressions of it are in your care, both in your local community and across the state. We encourage you to join us in working to protect what remains of Georgia's precious natural heritage.

FOREWORD

This book represents the completion of the first phase of a larger project entitled Still Small Voices: The Natural Environments of Georgia in Photographs, Poetry and Prose, based upon Dr. Charles H. Wharton's classic text, *The Natural Environments of Georgia.*

Dr. Wharton's book was one of the first in the nation to provide a comprehensive inventory of a state's natural environments. His study identified and described one hundred unique and distinct ecological communities in Georgia. To this day, Dr. Wharton's book remains the definitive text on Georgia's natural communities.

A research ecologist and Georgia State University professor, Dr. Wharton was a passionate advocate for the preservation of Georgia's unspoiled places. The late Dr. Eugene Odum, renowned University of Georgia professor known as the founder of modern ecology, said that Dr. Wharton "probably knows more about the natural areas of Georgia than any other person."

Dr. Wharton described the natural, cultural, and educational values of Georgia's native environments. His work led to the protection of many significant natural areas in this state. A dedicated scientist and educator, Dr. Wharton also recognized the spiritual and emotional impact that wild places have upon people. He cited many ways in which nature supports and enhances the quality of human life.

It was Dr. Wharton's "fervent hope" that his study would "gain recognition for the rapidly shrinking areas that represent the remaining splendor of our natural endowment." The full potential of his vision has yet to be realized. In the years since his study was published, many sites are believed to have suffered serious degradation, intrusion, or loss.

The Still Small Voices project reaches beyond the scientific community and presents Georgia's environments to a wider audience. It is our mission to give a voice to Georgia's wild places — to educate and inspire Georgians to recognize and protect the remnants of our state's natural heritage.

July 30, 2002

Dear Ann:

When I wrote the *Natural Environments of Georgia*, in cooperation with other scientists and officials of the Georgia Department of Natural Resources, I had to omit trying to express the thoughts and feelings inspired by the wild and beautiful places I tried to document.

The book that you and Marc Del Santro propose would fill this void, and thereby reach a much wider audience. The best outcome of an increased public awareness would be that it would assist the State and other organizations in preserving examples of our heritage. It would also help realize a dream of mine — a statewide system of educational natural areas for use by schools at all levels.

Hopefully, you and Marc can make an additional but less tangible contribution by interpreting the psychological and spiritual impact that these environments elicit. As you know, experiencing Nature can rise above self-indulgence in the unfettered joy of being in primeval surroundings, generating feelings that reach back through our long, long prehistoric past, when we daily dwelt in primordial environments of the earth.

May God bless your efforts to attest to his glorious creations.

Sincerely,

Charles Wharton
Affiliate Faculty

This letter was written by Dr. Charles H. Wharton, Affiliate Faculty, University of Georgia Institute of Ecology, in support of the Still Small Voices project.

INTRODUCTION

It is no accident that we met Dr. Wharton on Valentine's Day, for this project is a work of the heart. On February 14, 2002, photographer Marc Del Santro and I set out to meet the famed naturalist and professor. It was a long journey from Atlanta to reach his home, nestled against the forested mountains of the Nantahala Wilderness along the Upper Tallulah River in north-central Georgia.

Like Dorothy and the Lion going to meet the Wizard of Oz, we climbed the long steps leading to his front door. Copies of his book in hand, we sought his advice and hoped for his blessing upon this newly conceived project. He stood before us, a formidable figure, towering in height and reputation. Our nerves were quickly calmed however, as Dr. Wharton welcomed us with the warmth and hospitality of an old friend.

Dr. Wharton listened to our plans for the Still Small Voices project. I told him how I had received a copy of his book as an undergraduate environmental science major at Shorter College in 1980. The book was among my favorites. I always kept it close at hand and used it to research habitats at nature preserves and parks where I worked over the years.

Marc credits Dr. Wharton's book with helping him to become a better nature photographer, informing his understanding of processes and patterns within the mosaic of each natural community. After years of studying the book on an almost daily basis, both Marc and I are amazed that we still discover new information within its pages.

Like its author, *The Natural Environments of Georgia* has a quiet and unassuming personality with great depth under the surface. Filled with black and white photographs of unusual landscapes and detailed descriptions of intriguing environments, the tattered volume beckoned from my bookshelf like a treasure map. For many years I hoped that one day I would be able to visit all of these places. That day finally arrived.

Marc and I worked together in the early 1990s, documenting cultural and historic sites around the state. After being out of touch for several years, we realized that we were both ready to apply our respective crafts of photography and writing, combined with our environmental and outdoor skills training, to do our part to help protect Georgia's natural environments.

We created the Still Small Voices project, based on Dr. Wharton's book and using the art forms of photography, poetry, and prose, to give a voice to Georgia's wild places, championing not just their ecological value, but also their beauty and mysterious ability to touch and inspire the human soul.

Dr. Wharton was quick to encourage us. He recognized that his book was a scientific study, and stated in its introduction that it "was no place for the lyric prose that would adequately describe the incredible blue marl gorges of Clay County, the gigantic buttresses of the cypress of Ebenezer Creek, or the hoary beauty of the great birch forest on the north face of Brasstown Bald." We all agreed that it was time to create a place for that lyric prose.

Marc and I established well-defined parameters for the project. Our goal is to document Georgia's "*natural* environments," as described by Dr. Wharton, "as opposed to those created or altered by man," and to produce a representative image and written description of each natural community that is both scientifically accurate and artistically inspiring.

Locations were chosen to present each environment in as close to an original and pristine condition as possible. We also set out to interpret, as Dr. Wharton suggested, "the psychological and spiritual impact these environments elicit."

Much of Georgia's native landscape has been altered from its original condition by the effects of historical and modern land uses such as agriculture, timber harvesting, and urbanization. Amazingly, remnants of some native environments retain near-pristine conditions and harbor a diversity of plant and animal life that rivals that of the tropical rainforests.

With the help of the Non-Game Wildlife and Natural Heritage Section of the Georgia Department of Natural Resources and The Nature Conservancy, we identified and selected locations with the least amount of disturbance to provide a photograph that would serve as a classic example or "signature image" of each environment type.

The distribution and condition of Georgia's natural environments range from very rare and located in just a few places to more widespread, but often fragmented, locales. Some images in this book, such as the photographs of the Coosa Valley Prairies, record the only known location of that type of environment that remains in our state.

Some altered environments will return to near-original condition if left alone. Others require human involvement. Reintroduction of natural fire cycles, restoration of hydrology, and removal of non-native invasive species are some of the management tools being employed to restore many of our state's natural environments.

After documenting the twenty-five environments presented here, and visiting dozens more, we agree with Dr. Wharton when he said, "During this study, after thirty years of field experience in this state, I have come upon environments that have left me profoundly incredulous."

We hope this journey through twenty-five of Georgia's natural environments renews your sense of wonder for what is native and inspires you to get involved in efforts to preserve and protect the remnants of our state's magnificent natural heritage.

Hydric Systems (water-controlled systems)

1	**Mountain and Piedmont Springs**
2	Coastal Plain Springs
3	Underground Aquifers
4	Wet Cliffs and Outcrops
5	**Mountain River**
6	Spring-Fed Stream
7	Blackwater River and Swamp System
8	**Blackwater Branch or Creek Swamp**
9	Alluvial River and Swamp System — Piedmont
10	**Alluvial River and Swamp System — Coastal Plain**
11	Coosa River and Swamp System
12	**Tidewater River and Swamp System**
13	Backwater Streams
14	River Marsh and Fresh Water Marsh
15	Smooth Cordgrass Marsh
16	Salt Grass Marsh
17	Needle Rush Marsh
18	Edge Zone
19	Brackish Marsh
20	Tidal Pool
21	Oligohaline Creek
22	Tidal Creek, Canal, and River
23	Estuaries and Sound
24	Oyster Reef
25	Beach
26	Cypress Pond
27	Gum Pond
28	Carolina Bays
29	Bay Swamp
30	**Bog Swamp** (Okefenokee)
31	**Cypress Savannah**
32	**Herb Bog** (Pitcherplant Bog)
33	Shrub Bog
34	**Mountain and Piedmont Bog; Spring Seep**

8

35	Limesink
36	**Sagpond**
37	Marsh Pond
38	Natural Levee Type
39	Beaver Dam Type

Mesic to Xeric Systems (moist-to-dry land systems)

Cumberland Plateau and Ridge and Valley Provinces

40	**Bluff and Ravine Forest**
41	Forests on Colluvial Flats
42	Submesic Ridge and Slope Forest
43	Forest of Chickamauga Valley
44	Deciduous Forest of the Great Valley
45	**Ravine, Gorge and Cove Forest**
46	Oak-Pine Forest of the Great Valley
47	**Armuchee Ridge Forest**
48	**Cedar Glades**
49a	**Coosa Valley Prairies — Wet Prairie**
49b	**Coosa Valley Prairies — Dry Prairie**
50	**Rock Outcrops**
51	Caves

Blue Ridge Province

52	Broadleaf Deciduous Cove Forest
53	**Boulderfields**
54	**Oak Ridge Forest**
55	Chestnut Ridge Forest
56	Chestnut Oak Ridge Forest
57	Oak-Chestnut-Hickory Forest
58	Shrub Bald
59	Broadleaf Deciduous Ridge Forest
60	Broadleaf Deciduous-Hemlock Forest

9

Natural environments can be classified in a variety of ways, based upon the vast number of systems used to identify and organize them. The one hundred environments listed here were originally categorized and described in *The Natural Environments of Georgia* by Dr. Charles H. Wharton in 1978.

Some of these environments may be known by alternate names. Some may have been combined into broader categories or subdivided into more specific categories when described in other classification systems. Most of the names listed here, however, are still recognized and cross-referenced by field biologists and ecologists working in Georgia.

Environments 49a and 49b, the Coosa Valley Prairies, were discovered after the publication of Dr. Wharton's text. They are located in an area that was historically the range of the Coosa Flatwoods, a longleaf pine community described from historical records and listed as environment 49 in Wharton. There are no known examples of the Coosa Flatwoods still in existence.

The twenty-five environments highlighted in bold are represented in this book. It is our hope to document the additional seventy-five environments and present them in future volumes. See map on page 11 for locations of the featured environments.

**Physiographic Provinces
of Georgia**

Cumberland Plateau

Ridge and Valley

Blue Ridge

Piedmont

Upper Coastal Plain

Lower Coastal Plain

Hydric Systems (water-controlled systems)

1   Mountain and Piedmont Springs
5   Mountain River
8   Blackwater Branch or Creek Swamp
10 Alluvial River and Swamp System — Coastal Plain
12 Tidewater River and Swamp System
30 Bog Swamp (Okefenokee)
31 Cypress Savannah
32 Herb Bog (Pitcherplant Bog)
34 Mountain and Piedmont Bog; Spring Seep
36 Sagpond

Mesic to Xeric Systems (moist-to-dry land systems)

40 Bluff and Ravine Forest
45 Ravine, Gorge, and Cove Forest
47 Armuchee Ridge Forest
48 Cedar Glades
49a Coosa Valley Prairies — Wet Prairie
49b Coosa Valley Prairies — Dry Prairie
50 Rock Outcrops — Cumberland Plateau

53 Boulderfields
54 Oak Ridge Forest

68 Oak-Hickory Climax Forest
76 Rock Outcrops — Piedmont

86 Dwarf Oak-Evergreen Shrub Forest
88 Maritime Strand Forest
89 Upland Maritime Forest
95 Longleaf Pine Upland Forest (Longleaf Pine-Wiregrass)

10

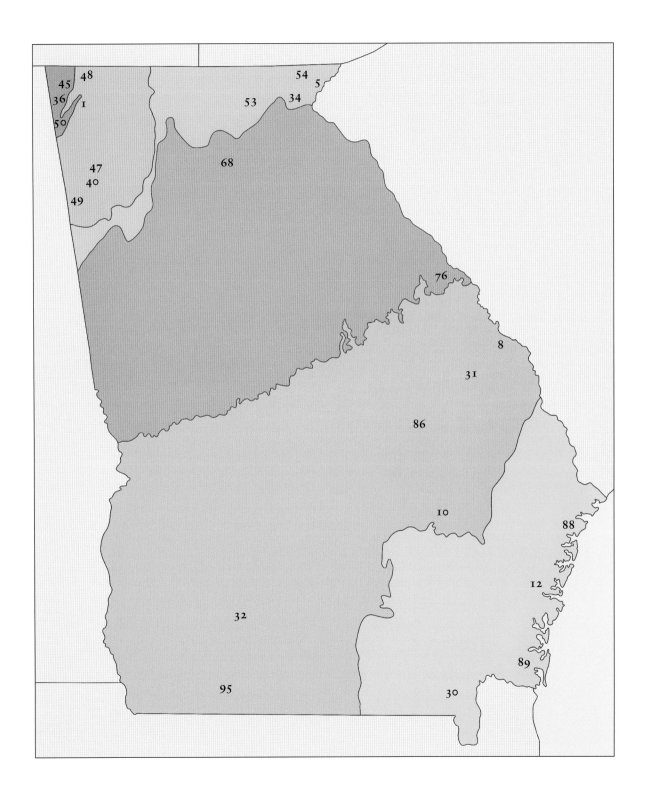

With still small voices they speak

in a language we may one day understand ...

Like a sage
clothed as a pauper,
    the spring's humble setting
belies its
    deep and mysterious
        nature.

MOUNTAIN AND PIEDMONT SPRINGS

Blue Hole Spring rests quietly at the end of an old road that winds along the base of Pigeon Mountain in northwest Georgia. Far from any big city, but not remote, Blue Hole is one of the few mountain springs of its size that remains unaltered by the addition of man-made structures.

Like a sage clothed as a pauper, the spring's humble setting belies its deep and mysterious nature. A cloak of cold, dense air, created by the water's constant fifty-six-degree temperature, hangs heavily over the spring. Passing through this invisible curtain washes the grime of city-thinking from our minds.

Standing at the edge of the natural limestone rocks from which the spring emerges, we slowly awaken to the subtle wonders of Blue Hole and its surroundings — the fragile anatomy of fossils locked in stone, water cold to the touch, and apparitions of small fish darting like shafts of light among the shadows.

At this spring, an abundance of cool, clean water flows, surfacing from a labyrinth of caves under the mountain. Devoid of sediment or organic matter that would alter its color, the water contained in the pool remains translucent blue, revealing a shallow, sandy bottom and the dark entrance to its source.

The water's surface makes holograms of the mountains, the trees, and the ever-changing sky, blurring the distinction between what is reflection and what is real, what is superficial and what is depth.

Like the tiny snails that thrive in this pure water, we stretch from the safety of our shells, emerging to gaze deeper into the spring to see what it contains and find there a beautiful blue map of the soul.

Sit beside a mountain spring,
where the water greets the sky.
Do not be in a hurry to go.
Linger longer,
for this is a place of creation —
clear, cold, refreshing, and pure —
sometimes seemingly still,
but always a fountain flowing,
pouring forth from the sand and stone,
rising from the sheltered safety
of Earth's rocky chambers,
surfacing from a journey eons long,
singing, saying:
Drink.

In a flash,
        a smooth, dark tail
    rises in a curve from the water
                and disappears —
    a lithe body
            taking itself out
of timelessness
                for a brief
                    moment.

MOUNTAIN RIVER

Over the deep valleys and gorges of northeast Georgia, the sun breaks late through the morning fog. Far below, like a silver ribbon reflecting the sky, a river cuts its way through rocky terrain. An hour-long descent on a winding trail through a dry ridge-forest of oak and pine leads us to one of the last untamed rivers in the eastern United States. Like a high, steady wind, the river's roar rises through the trees, announcing its presence, daring us to venture closer.

Our pace is soon slowed by the soft, dark hush of a hemlock grove and deep green thickets of rhododendron and mountain laurel that guard the river's edge. Raindrops soak in slowly, and the smell of wet soil lingers in the air like incense. A fragile web of wildflowers, shrubs, and tree roots is all that holds this living reservoir of soil on the steep mountain slopes.

Rivulets form small streams that dance down rocky slopes, merging in the ravines to form mighty rivers. Great volumes of water pour through narrow gorges in continuous waves that rise and fold over giant boulders, plunging between the rocks and resurfacing in synchronized bursts of sparkling spray.

Cascading down waterfalls, drumming and pounding as it passes, the river stirs itself, gaining oxygen that is long-held by the ice-cold water. This pleases the trout and the cadres of fly larvae the fishes love to consume.

Where the river widens, the water slows and drops its sediment, forming beaches of deep white sand — welcome way stations on the river's long journey to the coastal plain.

Beautiful but unforgiving, with as many moods as the sea, the mountain river changes quickly from black to olive to turquoise, moving as swiftly as the clouds that pass overhead. In a flash, a smooth, dark tail rises in a curve from the water and disappears — a lithe body taking itself out of timelessness for a brief moment. Was it a trout? An otter? Or was it a nymph — a spirit of nature that will live on only as long as the river is wild?

A mountain river
moves with a mission:

to shape the Earth
and alter its course.

With unleashed intention
she moves mountains.

With abandon she rolls over the rocks

and splashes her exhilaration
on those who stand ready to be moved.

She can take forever —
there is no hurry with her,

for she has been granted the gift of time.

Look what she has done so far.
Imagine what she will do.

21

The sound rises
and dives
like a dolphin
communicating
from the distant sea,
reminding us
that the land and the water
are connected
and that what may seem far away
is really quite near.

BLACKWATER BRANCH OR CREEK SWAMP

In the green light of early spring in South Georgia's Coastal Plain, a catfish glides through a blackwater branch, searching for a place to spawn. Through marmalade-colored water he cuts a slalom course over sugar-white sand, winding between the cones of the wide-bottomed cypress trees. As he disappears into the shadows, water sparkling like gold in his wake, we turn to plot our own course through the creek swamp.

A dark carpet of decaying leaves and fallen limbs defines the narrow floodplain, still saturated and draining from the creek's most recent rising. The air is sweet with the new leaves of maple, ironwood, water oak, and tupelo trees that camp along these blackwater lowlands. River cane and palmetto are just beginning to sprout, and the forest appears open and inviting.

Following the tracks of a five-fingered night bandit, we make our way to the creek bank. Mosquitoes, voracious the day before, are tamed by a constant breeze, granting us the luxury of time without their torture. Water swirls in small eddies around racks of humus and leaf litter caught in the web-like branches of fallen trees.

Over this flat land we can see the stream as it meanders deep into the swamp, gleaming in the sunlight with each bend on its way to the blackwater river and the sea. It is tempting to follow without caution, but we must stay alert. The ground is slippery and riddled with the piercing spires of cypress knees, and there are other hidden dangers.

The solid trunk of a tupelo tree serves as an anchor and offers a safe place to rest as we watch for what lies within the swamp, wondering about its fragility and its fate. These wooded wetlands are a last bastion for songbirds, singing frogs, turtles, snakes, and owls; a breeding and feeding ground for fish; and a natural way to filter the water and replenish the land in a graceful exchange that sustains us all.

As the wind picks up, two trees lean and sway together releasing a strange high-pitched whine. The sound rises and dives like a dolphin communicating from the distant sea, reminding us that the land and the water are connected and that what may seem far away is really quite near.

Springs break forth from the sandy ground,
joining courses of the rain,
creating the branches and creek swamps
of the sandy coastal plain.

Veils of yellow, green, and gold
shimmer as she bends
and weaves her way among the cypress trees
in the circle she works to mend.

Her ways are clear, not simple —
an advanced chemistry
of cleansing water and nourishing soils
in dark swamps of mystery.

Observe the turtles, full of eggs,
if you want to understand.
For them there are no boundaries
between the water and the land.

24

The trees are quiet,
and though they have a
watchful presence,
they seem preoccupied,
as if convened
in a secret meeting to discuss
the sacred knowledge
only those who have attained
five centuries
can comprehend.

ALLUVIAL RIVER AND SWAMP SYSTEM —
COASTAL PLAIN

When one thinks of primeval forests, most often it is the redwood, sequoia, or bristlecone pine that comes to mind. But in Georgia's alluvial river and swamp systems of the Coastal Plain, the long-lived survivors are the bald cypress and water tupelo, some reaching to six hundred years and others more than a thousand years of age. On a first visit to one of Georgia's last remaining old-growth bottomland hardwood forests, we fall under the spell of its ancient architecture.

Just out of sight of the Altamaha River, we wander in silence down the corridor of swamp. It is late July and the saturated soil barely supports our weight. Over slick mud and decaying leaves, on land that belongs to the river, we step cautiously, feeling like Jack in the giant's castle, sensing the imminence of the master's return.

Awed by the stature of its great trees, we must stay alert to avoid the spears of cypress knees that jut out like spikes guarding a well-defended outpost. Watermarks stain the trees above the wide buttresses, more than twelve feet from the ground, indicating the great volume of water these natural reservoirs can contain. The storms of hurricane season have not yet come, but the trees wait, knowing the river will rise again.

An alluvium of silt, sand, and clay carried by floodwaters is deposited here. The trees and other plants clean the water by filtering pollutants and absorbing the natural and man-made chemicals in the alluvium. Fish spawn among the flooded trees, and countless other creatures find food and sanctuary.

The trees are quiet, and though they have a watchful presence, they seem preoccupied, as if convened in a secret meeting to discuss the sacred knowledge only those who have attained five centuries can comprehend. Will we learn to accept their wisdom and come to appreciate all that they give? Or will we ignore them, as we have done so many times in the past, only to regret it in the end?

Take your hat off here
to the forest primeval,
to the river's meander,
and the flood.

Take your hat off here
to the lean and sway,
to the anchored,
and the hurricanes.

Take your hat off here
to nature's great clock,
to longevity that lingers
and paces the world.

Take your hat off here
to languages long forgotten,
to the stage set,
and dramas yet to come.

Just as the heart
circulates blood
to the body's extremities,
the work of this wetland
reaches far
beyond its borders.

TIDEWATER RIVER AND SWAMP SYSTEM

Deep in the Georgia delta, many miles upriver from the saltwater sea, it is the time between the tides, that brief moment when the rivers and creeks are full, and all is still. In the narrow shade of a cypress tree, a small alligator drifts by, his eyes rising just above the dark water. A heron stretches her wings, unaffected, and returns to resting.

This is the tidewater river and swamp system, the remnants of a once-vast, forested wetland that spanned the lower coastal regions of the southeastern United States. This lush realm of cypress and water tupelo, edged in freshwater gardens of pickerel weed, wild rice, and water lilies, is a last refuge for hundreds of species of rare and endangered plants and animals.

As the tide turns, the water races out toward the distant ocean, obedient to the moon's demands. In just a few hours, only a trickle remains in the stream beds, exposing dark brown mud, roots, and cypress knees. Twice each day, in a powerful exchange, the land receives the river's overflow and its mineral-rich sediments, and in return, sends the waters back cleansed and full of nutrients.

This action of the tides was once used for a great-but-fleeting profit as the cypress and gum swamps were cleared and drained, and the tidal rivers were channeled to flood rice plantations. Today, conversion of these wetlands for human uses continues, and chemical laden run-off from upstream land use finds its way into this fragile eco-system.

These wetlands are vestiges of hope for much of our native wildlife — insects, amphibians, reptiles, mammals, and birds.

The saltwater nurseries for sea-life depend upon this wetland's freshwater pulses. Just as the heart circulates blood to the body's extremities, the work of this wetland reaches far beyond its borders. From receiving and purifying upland floodwaters to feeding the life of the sea, its influence reaches from the ocean to our very doorstep.

The river waits
before entering the sea,
bows,
and pours black tea
into carved cups of land.

It's a hearty blend —
heat-steeped and stained
with what seeps from leaves and trees.

Much is arranged
in this ceremony,
supervised by the moon:

the ocean receives
blessings —
gifts of fish,
fresh water,
flowers, and wild rice —

and is pleased
with the exchange

and the river
fulfills her destiny.

32

From high in the sky,
    their trumpeting stirs
                a restlessness,
            like a longing
        for a home
34
that one has yet to find.

BOG SWAMP (OKEFENOKEE)

Just as autumn begins to take hold in Georgia, migrating sandhill cranes pass overhead in classic formation, heralding the coming of winter. From high in the sky, their trumpeting stirs a restlessness, like a longing for a home that one has yet to find. Traveling hundreds of miles southward, we follow the cranes and find them feeding and nesting deep in the prairies of the largest bog swamp in Georgia — the Okefenokee Swamp.

When thinking of swamps, one imagines tea-colored water and winding passageways through cypress trees draped in Spanish moss. But this bog swamp is much more. It is a mosaic of floating islands of peat, grasslands, thickets of myrtle and bay, and forests of cypress and water tupelo.

On a long boardwalk that leads deep into the swamp, we pass by blooms of yellow-eyed grass nestled in bowls of dark green mosses. Pinstriped pitcherplants hide in the shadows, and ferns, backlit by the sun, thrive in this blackwater garden. At last we reach the wide-open prairie as it presses into an indigo lake. Lightning fires have kept these prairies open, and patches of water lilies lead the eye to the horizon.

Two sandhill cranes fly in, make a wide circle, then settle against a wall of shrubs in a sea of tall grasses. For a time our restlessness ceases, and we, too, feel at home.

We need wilderness
in this world,

places to wander for days
and never cease to wonder.

We need vast open spaces
where the wind sings
a different kind of song,

known to those who travel far
to find a home,
like the crane,
Earth's most ancient of birds.

We need swamps
and bogs where water flows in sheets
and gives birth to rivers,

where lightening leaps
and fires smolder for seasons.

We need springs and streams
where we can feed and drink deeply
from a well
we have almost forgotten.

We need wilderness,
for it is the resting place of our dreams.
It keeps them safe
until it is time for them to fly.

*... a presence is palpable
and seems to acknowledge
that we are here.*

CYPRESS SAVANNAH

Far from any urban outpost, deep in the heart of southeast Georgia, the cypress savannah stands as one of the South's grand but vanishing wetland environments. Once widespread, many of these water-filled lowlands have been lost over the years to logging, draining, and fire suppression.

Under a blue August sky, a company of botanists hikes in search of *Oxypolis canbyi*, a federally endangered flower that makes its home on the edge of the cypress savannah. As if on safari, we pass through the tall, dry grasses like a slow-moving caravan under a canopy of longleaf pine. As the land slopes downward, the pines fade behind us. The grass becomes greener and the soil seeps underfoot. In winter, we would be walking here in chest-high water, but in this drier time of year, we are granted easy passage.

In the cypress savannah, a presence is palpable and seems to acknowledge that we are here. There are no signs of alligators, but still we watch. The cypress trees are graciously spaced, and there is no understory, so the view is vast and open. Among the myrtle and fern, healthy young cypresses sprout. A frog lends color to a patch of grey bark, with his yellow-brown legs and luminescent body of green.

The group divides into small parties, each following its own pursuits. A few stay behind in the center of the savannah, where the wide buttresses of the pond cypress provide a solid place to lean after a long, hot trek.

Looking up the length of their textured trunks, we see white clouds rushing by and needled branches brushing the sky with wide circling strokes. In this solitude, we are not alone. Wood storks nest here in the highest branches and egrets make simple homes in lower shrubs nearby. Dragonflies dart and shimmer, reminding us that there are creatures still with us from Earth's more ancient days.

As the sun sets, we leave the long shadows of the savannah behind. At last we find a solitary stalk of *O. canbyi*, its long stem tipping under the weight of its lace-like blossom. The company lets out a soft cheer, celebrating a small victory in the battle to save a species, perhaps sensing we are saving a part of ourselves that we have not yet come to know.

Time is an alligator —
belly to the earth —
watching dragonflies
dart across the millennia.

Time swims
in a slow, steady glide,
swallowing epochs like afternoons,

then lifts itself
suddenly
and catches us unaware.

Time crawls among the cypress trees,
the conifer, and fern —
still here from the days of the dinosaurs.
Now, from them, we can learn.

Time sees how with heavy footsteps,
the great ones rose, then fell.
Will we do things differently?
Only time will tell.

In a burst
of visual harmony,
trumpet pitcherplants
tone in unison
with a sound
that resonates
through the corridors
of the soul.

HERB BOG (PITCHERPLANT BOG)

On an April afternoon, in the far reaches of southwest Georgia, we go in search of one of the best examples of the state's last remaining herb bogs, more commonly known as pitcherplant bogs. From the ridges of pine that surround them, the bogs are difficult to spot, and we must walk down-slope through fields of wiregrass to find them. A patch of vibrant green comes into view, and we find the elusive wetland lying nestled in a wide swale that drains the surrounding hillsides.

An herb bog is something to behold. We follow the paths of the animals through this unusual wetland, careful not to step on the stalks and blooms of a host of carnivorous plants. Hooded pitcherplants nod over bonneted yellow blossoms; parrot pitcherplants lean back in lazy circles; and sundew smile open-mouthed with drops of nectar glistening from their tiny teeth. In a burst of visual harmony, trumpet pitcherplants tone in unison with a sound that resonates through the corridors of the soul.

When natural fires sweep through, they clear the woody brush and renew the land like a revival. From a fragile alchemy of dark, acidic soil, a succession of countless herbs and grasses sprout and bloom here from spring through fall. Suppression of fire, along with disturbances such as ditching, draining, and plant collecting, has led to the demise of all but a few herb bogs in Georgia.

This shallow bowl provides a strategic vantage point from which to view the surrounding uplands. A few tall pitcherplants stand like sentries on the outskirts of the bog, noting who comes and goes. With still small voices they speak — in a language we may one day understand.

The Earth has a choir

and voices
bellowing like green frogs in the night —
each vocalizing its own desires.

But in the choir
there is unity,

and *that* is different.

When each sings as a part of a whole
in recognition of a great goodness,

that is how things will be made right.

44

45

In this moment,
I am certain
that it is the cultivation
of tenderness,
fierce hope,
and dedication
that will safeguard
and restore
these
mountain treasures.

MOUNTAIN AND PIEDMONT BOG; SPRING SEEP

High above a narrow river valley of the eastern Blue Ridge is one of only a few known mountain bogs remaining in the state of Georgia. It is a long, rugged hike to reach this remote and rare environment. We pause often for water, to catch our breath, and to listen to the distant rustle in the trees. This is the land of the raven and the bear.

At the summit, the trail levels to a wide, open wood. Stepping cautiously through the dry leaves under a canopy of weathered oaks and knee-high huckleberry bushes, we spot the entrance to our destination, a dark green thicket of mountain laurel. Its woven branches bend and twist to form a fairy-like labyrinth through which we must navigate to reach the bog.

A mountain bog is formed near a spring that seeps over flat land or where rainwater is held in a depression in mountainous terrain. The shallow current spreads and soaks into the rich, forest soil, making a soggy, muddy home for bog turtles, salamanders, pitcherplants, and other rare species. The North Georgia mountains were once dotted with dozens of pitcherplant bogs. Through habitat loss, plant-collecting, and perhaps the removal of beaver, all but a few have been destroyed.

Shining like a happy child who is unaware of any threats to her existence, the shallow water sparkles in the noonday sun, weaving through thick mats of peat moss and purple pitcherplants.

In the growing shadows of late afternoon, the bog darkens to a deep, mysterious blue. A small, orange salamander surfaces and is placed carefully in my hand. In this moment, I am certain that it is the cultivation of tenderness, fierce hope, and dedication that will safeguard and restore these mountain treasures.

Her waters weave through sand and sedge —
bright daylight — trumpets glow.
Pitcher plants play hide and seek
where silky grasses grow.

On neighboring mountains her kin are gone —
what danger she does not know.
How precious this rare child becomes
when too soon her days may go.

In her shadows she is darkness
and a galaxy of stars,
reflecting the deep blue mystery
of all we've been and are.

48

As *darkness* settles in
after a long day of *rain*,
a box turtle
hides in plain sight
and the frogs
are at *peace*.

SAGPOND

When fall's first blush reddens the sourwood and the hawthorn have gone to seed, the trees, still leafed, keep watch over their secret places. Hundreds of these small but vital wetlands — known simply as sagponds — form in sinks of the sandstone and limestone bedrock of northwest Georgia. These mysterious vernal pools glow like emerald cities hidden deep in the forest, guarded only by the woods that surround them and by the creatures they shelter.

Each sagpond is unique in its arrangement and a community unto itself. Some host only sedges, while others display tall tussocks of grasses cohabitating with sphagnum mosses, ferns, fungi, and a host of colorful shrubs. Only trees born to the wetlands, such as red maple, swamp tupelo, and willow oak, gather in groves nearby.

With fluctuating water levels, the sagponds are a refugia for some species of plants found more commonly in the coastal plain, and fossilized pollen reveals secrets of life here long ago. The humus is rich, dark, and matted with roots and leaves slowly decaying. To press upon it is to feel a soft return — firm, but giving — like the handshake of a trusted friend.

The water enters not by land, but is granted by the rain and stays, sinking into the earth over many days. Wildlife drinks here in times of drought, and waterfowl gather to rest and to taste the seeds of the button bush.

As darkness settles in after a long day of rain, a box turtle hides in plain sight and the frogs are at peace. A banded water snake moves out of the pond with purpose. Will we join him in keeping watch over these places, and find a way to keep them safe, or will they disappear like another Avalon, lost without a trace?

Have you ever stepped into the office
of a kind professor?

Stepped through, and known Welcome?

Patience and a pipe, an open door?

How often do we find this —
someone whose presence is a pond?

Someone who knows that knowledge grows by nature,
not by force?

Stop here a while,
where the waters are still
but not stagnant.

What has come before
still lingers here.

From just a small sample,
one can find
deep knowledge.

There is a relationship between the land
and those who love it.

Come and sit,
and when it is time,
move along.

It is the way of things.

54

Like libraries,
these forests
reveal their secrets slowly
to those who venture in,
seek the quiet corners,
and stay
to leaf through
the long unopened pages.

BLUFF AND RAVINE FOREST

Anchored on dramatic slopes that rise above the rivers of northwest Georgia, the bluff and ravine forests are living testaments to the original bounty of this state's natural heritage. Often north-facing, densely shaded, and too steep for extensive logging and farming, these forests retain their native soils and are rich with botanical treasures.

In late winter, we make our way through a narrow ravine, hoping to catch the woods' early awakening. The land rises steeply to the east and to the west, bridged only by fallen trees that lie across the stream like massive moss-covered cannons. The bedrock, eons old, has crumbled into rubble. As unstable as a mountain of gravel, the sliding hillside challenges the knees and ankles to a day-long duel with unsure footing. The soil is rich, but thinly scattered like last year's leaves, and is easily disturbed and pushed down-slope.

In a few weeks, the woods will become lush with an alphabet of small, early wildflowers. Irises, trout lilies, violets, and windflower are just a few of the many forbs that peek up from these fern-shaded groves. Like the monks who curated mankind's earliest written documents, the bluff and ravine forests harbor a pharmacopoeia of ancient knowledge.

Shagbark hickory and northern red oak are among the many species of trees that share the canopy with hackberry and chestnut oak. An understory of silverbell, mock-orange, and hydrangea decorates the slopes. Like libraries, these forests reveal their secrets slowly to those who venture in, seek the quiet corners, and stay to leaf through the long-unopened pages. One always finds surprises and departs with more than the answers being sought.

At last we reach the bluff — its rocky outcrops jutting like jaws set defiantly against the north wind. Elegant beeches and maples with smooth, grey bark hold fast to their faded foliage, waiting for what the future may bring. As we look across the bare forest to the distant ridges beyond the river, a wild turkey sounds his call. Hearing no answer, he flies low and away. As he disappears over the bluff, we wonder, will he find sanctuary in the next ravine?

The ravines
are waiting
with some trepidation
about what the spring will bring.

Once they slept well in winter,
dreaming of hydrangea blooming
and lady fern unfolding.

Now, they rest with one eye open.

They have heard the tales
of trees falling
and land-clearing
and wonder:

Will they be next?

A butterfly
lives out the fullness of her life
in a few short beats.
At the edge
of the canyon
we can see millions of years
in one day.

RAVINE, GORGE, AND COVE FOREST

From the edges of ravines carved deep into the sandstone mountains of Georgia's Cumberland Plateau, one can see wide expanses of sheer cliffs extending the length of long valleys. Echoes of a shallow roar rise up through the quiet of the gorge, more than one thousand feet below, where small streams labor as they have for millions of years, cutting through the sandstone, shale, and limestone layers of this ancient shoreline. From dry ridge-tops to moister bottom-slopes, these deep, narrow passes support the ravine, gorge, and cove forests — communities hardy enough to thrive in a land of contrasts.

On dry ledges, shortleaf and Virginia pine defy gravity as they stretch boldly beyond the safety of the rock. Within just a few feet, on the wetter, talus slopes, a colluvium of shale and limestone rubble collects and is home to moisture-loving hardwoods and hemlock near the streams.

Each autumn, ridge tops and slopes are softened by a quilt of golden-yellow tulip poplars, flaming orange hickories, and blood-red maples. For just one day it is perfect, and then a wind rises up the valley and shakes the blanket, freeing the leaves to drift and shimmer like ticker tape in a long, slow shower down through the gorge.

Passing over the narrow paths that wind along the edge of the steep-walled canyons, we rub shoulders against the roots of these hardy trees. Each switchback gives intimate views of the natural communities of a ravine, gorge, and cove forest. Mosses make themselves at home on the rock walls; strands of partridge berry hang like beaded curtains before small caves; and at the base of the gorge, massive boulders iced in pale-green lichens strike frozen poses with great personality.

Footing is uncertain on steep inclines and slippery rocks. Waterfalls spill into curved bowls cut into the canyon walls, making cozy amphitheatres where one can pause and listen to the splashing of water on the rocks and wonder about the different ways to measure time. On the slopes, the trees hold on for centuries. A butterfly lives out the fullness of her life in a few short beats. At the edge of the canyon, we can see millions of years in one day.

Stand at the edge of
time unfolding — a canyon
shrouded in the mist.

Hear the haunting voice
of the wind, brewing, stirring,
giving birth to clouds.

See how the ledge of
the moment is built on an
abundance of days.

60

Gravity,
our ever-present
traveling companion,
stands ready
to take advantage
of any
careless move.

ARMUCHEE RIDGE FOREST

The Armuchee Ridges rise like a miniature mountain range between the great valleys of northwest Georgia, glowing lavender and blue in the light of a setting sun. From a distance they appear uniform, but each ridge bears its own peculiar tilt or fold of limestone, sandstone, shale, or chert, giving birth to forest communities that defy simple classification.

On a late winter day, we enter the Marshall Forest to photograph one of the best examples of an Armuchee Ridge forest in the region. Bundled against the cold and weighted down with camera gear, we quickly discover that these forests are more rugged than they appear. Just yards from a well-traveled road, civilization feels far away.

Steep walls rise up on either side, creating a valley so narrow there is barely enough room for a trail. Casualty of a recent storm, a giant tree more than ten feet in circumference blocks the way. Surveying the mass of branches, small trees, and vines taken down with it, we choose to go around, hoisting ourselves up the side of a near-vertical slope. The rocky ground gives way with each step as we grasp for handholds among small saplings and roots. Gravity, our ever-present traveling companion, stands ready to take advantage of any careless move.

Halfway up the ridge, we pause to recover both breath and balance. From this vantage point we can see the great diversity of trees that characterize the Armuchee Ridge forests. Different species of oaks and hickories along with a variety of large pines make their home here. Longleaf pine approaches its northern limits in the state, and northern red oak reaches the southern extent of its range. In springtime, dogwood and redbud will dress up the understory, and in early summer, a threatened mountain mint will bloom in the safety of this refuge.

A hawk flies in low and whistles a shrill report. Ushered on by his call, we scramble down the hillside and at last reach the end of the trail. A massive pine stands like a sentry, guarding the entrance to the ridges beyond. This elder of the woods embodies the longevity and tenacity of these forests and serves as the subject of our photograph. Laden with tales of two centuries, it waits patiently for those who will venture in to discover its many secrets.

Armuchee Ridge forests,
self-contained,
keep close
what no one has seen:

the time deemed
to reveal themselves

as upright shields,
steadfast providers,
storehouses of integrity,
and keepers of hope.

Visited by catastrophe,
they survive great losses,
harboring seeds —
the future guardians
when the great ones fall.

So sanctioned,
they serve us well.

64

Open to both
earth and sky,
one can almost hear
the quiet conversations
of those
who passed here
before.

CEDAR GLADES

Hidden within the hardwood forests of the Chickamauga Valley, one of Georgia's most rare natural environments waits quietly and seems pleased to receive the company of visitors. After a short trek through a forest of oak and pine, thick with saplings, shrubs, and vines, the crackling sound of twigs and leaves underfoot abruptly ends and we find ourselves in the bright opening of a cedar glade.

Wide platforms of slate-gray limestone bedrock breach the surface here and become broken and scattered into long gravel washes that run the length of the long, narrow glade. Cedars of all ages are staged randomly about the rocky grassland like lampposts in a city park. Wildflowers inhabit the otherwise barren pathways, forming patchwork prairies amidst the rubble.

Edged in lush green mosses, the cedar glades are like walled gardens: private, quiet, and amenable to contemplation. Open to both earth and sky, one can almost hear the quiet conversations of those who passed here before, as they gathered to rest beside the wet-weather streams or gazed up at the stars.

These glades were created not by man, but by a soil too harsh for trees — other than the hardy red cedar. They are kept clear of invasive shrubs and saplings by the natural cycles of periodic fire. Saturated in winter and spring and very dry in the summer, the soil's climate is as harsh as pavement. Only the limestone-loving cedars and specially adapted herbs and grasses can thrive. Five hundred different species — nineteen found only in this habitat — have been discovered in the cedar glades.

As the sun drops behind the surrounding forest, a breeze finds its way into the glade and rustles the dried grasses. Soft-petaled flowers in purple, orange, yellow, and blue dream of the vast prairies farther to the west. A deer draws near and then slips quietly back into the dark woods. These glades have a purpose beyond what we can see. We must take care of them or like the deer they, too, may slip away.

There is a generation coming
that will seek out the forgotten places,
secure the last traces,
and lift long shadows from the land.

On foundations of knowledge
they will stand.

Renewing with fire,
holding back what seeks to stop them,

they will see the glades bloom once again.

One instinctively
walks carefully
and whispers here,
as if in the presence
of something
that might too quickly
disappear.

COOSA VALLEY PRAIRIES — WET PRAIRIE

This small paradise, hidden in the vast pine forests of northwest Georgia, is home to the rare whorled sunflower. This long-lost species was last seen more than one hundred years ago in Tennessee and was recently found in the Coosa Valley Prairie by a local botanist on a field trip with the Georgia Botanical Society.

With leaves like windswept hula skirts spinning up the length of its towering six-foot stalk, the whorled sunflower reigns over this wetland. From buds held tightly through mid-summer, swelling until ready to bloom in August, its bright yellow rays burst open to form flowers the size of silver dollars, nodding over the lush wet meadow below.

At just a fraction of its original size, the wet prairie is encircled by pines and a pressing succession of sweetgum trees and rattan vines. Its fragile and delicate nature is evident. One instinctively walks carefully and whispers here, as if in the presence of something that might too quickly disappear.

The Coosa Valley prairies are a part of a wider quilt of wooded uplands that includes post oaks and shortleaf and longleaf pines. Under natural conditions, fires spreading down-slope keep the prairies clear of encroaching woody vegetation.

Tucked neatly into the wet soil, fine stalks of rare sedges nestle among the larger mounds of grasses and huge wing-like leaves of prairie dock. From the dock's wide fans spring its yellow flowers, perched atop a tall stem. Like solar panels, the wide leaves of the dock provide a warm platform for the awakening creatures of the morning — on this day, grasshoppers, dragonflies, and green tree frogs.

When the world is wet and waking;
dew and mist are overtaking,
I sit low among the flowers,
close to the mud and grasses,
and come to love this place.

What is rare finds life here,
and flowers long forgotten are found.

There is a spirit that renews,
that speaks with the ancient sky,
and remembers days —
a force both young and old that waits.

While all around life moves on,
here it stays.

If strength and goodness
have a place,
it is here.

Here is their place.

The summer day warms to grasshoppers,
dragonflies, and a slick green frog.

Around and about, the forest can come no farther.
This prairie makes a stand.

72

The Coosa Valley Prairies
stand like pioneers
holding their claims
to a territory
that has long since
changed hands.

COOSA VALLEY PRAIRIES —
DRY PRAIRIE

Deep in the countryside west of Rome, Georgia, the Coosa Valley Prairies stand like pioneers holding their claims to a territory that has long since changed hands. On a dirt road that leads to this remnant prairie, sparks of color leap from the ditches, waking the weary eye with a radiant display of native wildflowers. Flashes of red, purple, and gold hint at what lies ahead as the resplendent blooms of cardinal flower, blazing star, and goldenrod herald the way to the prairies.

From a distance, the open hillside — nicknamed the Grand Prairie — shows off its graceful contours and gives the impression of hosting a thick carpet of blooms. But nearing, one sees that the flowers and grasses are well-spaced.

Tenacious prairie plants take root between cracked tablets of limestone and chert. The meager soil is too harsh for trees — even the hardy loblolly. Cedar and pine concede the territory, and those few woody shrubs that gain a foothold are soon cleared out by the purging forces of fire.

Open to the elements, these natural meadows take the heat of the sun without respite all summer long. But the wildflowers thrive in these bright openings. Purple coneflowers dance with confidence in their pink and tattered skirts. Small white asters shine among them, and black-eyed Susans wait in the wings, holding the golden promise of the season yet to come.

On the horizon, white clouds billow and the birds settle down, surrendering to the hot afternoon. A great blue heron passes overhead in an otherwise empty sky. A witness to the truth, she knows the prairies will survive if we will but honor their claim.

The prairie is a land uplifting —
for in it there is a sense of forever.
Not empty or frightening,
but a soft infinity,
as if tended to by someone who cares,
who keeps an eye on things,
like a gardener
or a grandmother who sews small stitches in a calico quilt.

Sweet abundance!
Yet still so much work to be done.

Bees hum.
Butterflies lift and flutter.
Tiny ants patrol the hard ground.
Seeds self-sown on forsaken soil
turn to indigo, gold, and lace.
Birds stutter in wonder
at the pink-petaled skirts of the season's poised dancers.

The sky gazes with great pleasure upon this patch of earth
and sighs.

And the prairie knows,
and shows how it feels to be cherished.

One carries the memory
of this light
like an ember
that shows the way out
through the long shadows
of night,
and hopes the benevolence
that granted safe passage
remains
to the end of the trail.

ROCK OUTCROPS — CUMBERLAND PLATEAU

Lookout Mountain arches across northwest Georgia in a thirty-one-mile stretch between Alabama and Tennessee. Its sister to the south, Pigeon Mountain, splits off like a lone rib, creating a fertile valley between the two ridges where the warm air rises up in a long, exhaled breath.

Those who linger on the ridges catch glimpses of strange geometric patterns emerging from within the wooded landscape. Geodesic domes hug the earth like nests of fossilized dinosaur eggs, and parapets of sandstone towering three-stories high keep watch over all who pass this way.

These rocky outposts reveal clues to their ancient origin. An estuary once flowed here and left behind deep layers of fossil-laden sediment that hardened into sandstone and limestone. Over the millennia, the elements eroded the softer minerals, leaving a labyrinth of passageways through massive boulders. Traces of iron ore remain, coloring the rock faces in puzzling shapes that entice the mind to name them.

This is a land of lost cities, castle keeps, and courtyards. Exploring its hallways and chambers promises adventure, and voices seem to whisper like tower guards granting safe passage.

Exposed to the wind and the sun, only the hardiest plants survive on these rocks, including some from the Coastal Plain. Trees and shrubs on the outcrops are stunted and shaped like bonsai, and among the tangled shadows of witch alder and gooseberry, vultures and wood rats make their nests on rocky ledges.

Shaded corridors and crevices create their own climate, where one can find shelter from the heat. These cool havens host dish gardens dripping with moisture-loving mosses and ferns that cling to the rock with mats of roots in a rich but fragile humus.

As the sun sets, the rocks glow like lanterns turned up to a peak, and then slowly turned down again. One carries the memory of this light like an ember that shows the way out through the long shadows of night, hoping the benevolence that granted safe passage remains to the end of the trail.

In the last glow of the setting sun
watch the gnomon shadows
work their way across the face
of a crashing wave suspended.

Touch time's cemented circles
captured on a sandpaper surface.
Bask in the glow of something greater.

Sit in the counsel of the old ones.
Sit close to the land
and let your face be carved with dignity.

Know the one who made this
is not far, but dwells within,
and laughs with the joy of this creation.

A pileated woodpecker
sounds his call,
reminding us
that he is watching over
this sacred space,
where the spirits of the mighty,
the trees
that once stood long
on the mountains,
come to rest.

BOULDERFIELDS

When the deep cold of the Pleistocene Age glaciated half of the northern hemisphere, it reached with icy fingers far into the southlands, establishing outposts on the north-facing slopes of Georgia's highest mountains.
On peaks above 3,000 feet, the constant pressure of ice-wedging caused large pieces of rock to calve from the mountains. Boulders tumbled down-slope, coming to rest below the summits, creating boulderfields.

One may imagine an expanse of bare rocks over which to leap and scramble, like the glacier fields farther to the north, but these southern boulderfields are on steep terrain. Walking here is difficult. Slippery mosses coat the loose rubble, and hip-high ferns conceal the ground. Saturated almost to the point of liquid form, the rich, dark soil slips out from underfoot, its hold maintained only by the delicate roots of herbs and trees. But a slow, careful ascent provides a strategic vantage point from which to view the scene: a topiary battlefield of trees and rocks frozen in a graceful state of deconstruction. In this cool, moist place, mosses and lichens quickly shroud what falls.

In the gateway to this coliseum, gilded yellow birch and massive buckeye — trees more often seen in colder climates — stand guard. Dutchman's breeches, waterleaf, and trout lily unfurl the colorful banners of flora more commonly found farther to the north.

Unsuited to farming and difficult to log, the boulderfields have escaped the worst of the harvest that robbed other mountain areas of their native soils. Snow lingers late here, and from under the boulders, the silver voices of ice-cold streams sing a quiet requiem.

A pileated woodpecker sounds his call, reminding us that he is watching over this sacred space, where the spirits of the mighty, the trees that once stood long on the mountains, come to rest.

She makes her home in the rainforest,
but travels far and wide,
looking for places where time stands still,
and new life rises from that which has died.

Through me she passes as I perch on the edge
of the cove so like her home,
and for a moment I see the Earth through her eyes,
and with her I do roam.

She circles the globe like St. Nicholas,
riding on the wind,
and lingers in places that welcome her,
where she can sew, but need not mend.

Her gifts she shares; she is ancient and wise.
She is the life of all growing and green.
She renews herself in those who believe
in what is real but cannot be seen.

It is a healing place
where the veil
between the human
and the divine
is thinner,
the gulf
not so vast.

OAK RIDGE FOREST

Hiking in the higher elevations of the Georgia Blue Ridge, one can climb above a sunny day and enter the clouds. Heart and breath work hard to lift the body to this wooded summit where the oak ridge forest maintains dominion. On these high, narrow ridges the constant action of fog, wind, rain, and ice prune and shape the trees. Like dancers on a dark stage, thick-trunked oaks hold fast while bent and gnarled branches strike odd poses, waiting for the next gale to shake them.

Evergreen heaths of rhododendron and mountain laurel soften the sturdy forms of the oaks, giving welcomed shelter to birds and mammals of the mountains while helping to hold the soil. We move quietly here, like the animals, watchful and observant.

Where rocks are exposed we pause in a moment of brief sunshine, sitting close to the ground, enjoying the sweet scent of fine grasses, ferns, and wildflowers. On this ridge-top, in the company of the hardy oaks, the body seems to cease its constant demands and enters a simple state of being.

Thunder echoes in the wide, open spaces of the valley between the mountains. Clouds roll in quickly, entering every space between twig and branch and leaf, soaking the mosses and lichens. Hikers on the Appalachian Trail spend weeks, sometimes months, passing through these elegant and mysterious forests. It is a healing place where the veil between the human and the divine is thinner, the gulf not so vast.

A cold rain is carried in by the wind, and we are glad to have packed raincoats and sweaters. Hastened by stray lightning bolts that accompany the storm, we reluctantly turn to leave. A small bird appears from out of the fog and flies skyward, fading into the mist — a reminder that spirit and nature are not so far apart. They dwell together.

Come rich wind,
into our world so small,
into our strange, bent lives.

Take our oak arms dancing.

Rattle us to the root.
Force us to the rock.

Make us feel the fiber of our being.

Find us fertile.
Find us dreaming.

A mature
oak-hickory forest
bequeaths a richness
that only the aged
can give.

OAK-HICKORY CLIMAX FOREST

The oak-hickory forest once reigned over the Georgia Piedmont. Now, old-growth examples are rare, for settlers cleared these forests for timber, pasture, and cropland. When old fields are left fallow, however, within a century the oak-hickory forest returns to reclaim its throne.

In suburbs and still-rural places, white oak is queen of the ridge with towering hickory standing guard. A mature oak-hickory forest bequeaths a richness that only the aged can give. Dogwood and redbud grace the sub-canopy with colorful blooms, and sourwood and sassafras produce honey and hearty root tonic.

In springtime, small kingdoms awaken on the forest floor. Sunlight filters through budding branches, giving life to delicate wildflowers below.

In summer, a sleepy stillness hangs like a hammock from the trees. Even the air is green. As thunderstorms come crashing, winds whip like waves through the branches. This high home to squirrels and thoroughfare to owls and a rivalry of hawks and crows, is now possessed by higher forces. Brittle limbs surrender to gravity and become a feast for fungi and small creatures that turn the old wood into soil.

In autumn, the forest lays down its mast for all to feed upon — a bountiful harvest for squirrels, chipmunks, deer, and man. With a warm wave of color and a crackle underfoot, hickory's tangy scent fills the air. The smoky aroma of oaks calls to mind Thanksgiving gatherings and the giving of gifts.

In winter the trees are quiet, awaiting spring's return. This is the time for cold-weather walks in the woods. All this grace is in the oak-hickory forest, once ever-present, now elusive, yet always ready to return.

A walk in the woods is a solitary thing,
even in good company.
We must navigate our own path.
With our own eyes we must watch for
where to place the next step.

In the quiet the mind settles
and the senses come to life. We listen
and, with more than our ears, begin to hear.

The very skin awakens
as we return to the knowledge
that we are both predator and prey.

What crouches behind that tree?
What coils beneath that log?
What perches in the branches above?

Step, pause, listen. Step, pause, listen.
What do we hope to find?

Often, it is just a journey, purpose unknown,
placing ourselves in the path of the unexpected,
flexing fibers deep within.

A woodpecker's laughter shatters the silence
and we are returned to the twenty-first century.
But the ancient past is not far from us here.

Here
one feels like
a space explorer
witnessing
the colonization of life
on a barren
planet.

ROCK OUTCROPS — PIEDMONT

Hidden amongst the pines of the Georgia Piedmont lay patches of exposed granite, ranging from just a few feet wide to more than several hundred acres in size. The domes of rock heave under the blazing summer sun and recoil with the cutting cold of winter. Rain and wind continually etch and carve channels in the stone, creating small basins where tiny grains of sand settle. With little or no soil, few trees grow on the open mounds of rock, yet these granite outcrops support rare plant communities that are amazingly well adapted to surviving under harsh conditions.

The surface of the rock is creeping with a colorful crust of primitive plant matter. Here one feels like a space explorer witnessing the colonization of life on a barren planet. Brittle pods of blackened mosses wait for rains to wake them. Explosions of red and pink and white ignite the rock's shallow craters like storms of meteors as the crimson-colored stonecrop rises to its peak bloom.

Over time, soils develop in the sandy pools, supporting a succession of red sedum, purple spiderwort, and yellow groundsel. Carolina jessamine climbs among soft-tan grasses, prickly-pear cacti, and an occasional gnarled cedar. These natural plant communities form zones of texture and color, creating patterns and curves that please the eye and rival any garden designed by man.

An undisturbed outcrop is a living lesson in biological succession — how life adapts and thrives. Yet, of the thousands of granite outcrops that dot the Georgia Piedmont, only a few still exist in a pristine state. These botanical wonderlands are a paradox worth preserving: tenacious and fragile, hardy and delicate, long in the making, and so easily destroyed.

Be amazed:

A grand display made by rains,
etched and traced from granite to grains.

Lichens paint life on its face,
creating a way, making a base.

Summer sun blazes and bakes.
Winter wind pierces and takes.

Red maidens skate on glycerin lakes.
All is intact and in its place.

Plants decay, deep soil is made.
Enter this garden without a spade.

96

*The air is sweetly scented
like a vintage perfume
        and the lungs are
pleased to breathe deeply
    of the soothing vapors
            of rosemary, pine, and
rare

        woody-stemmed

                mints.*

DWARF OAK - EVERGREEN SHRUB FOREST

In the southeast Georgia countryside — where pavement has not yet come, and time, like the tortoise, blesses the earth with slow steps — the land rises to a rare environment called the Ohoopee Dunes. This dwarf oak-evergreen shrub forest is made of coarse river sands piled up by strong westerly winds of the Pleistocene Age.

Like the gardens of a grand estate, where each plant is carefully chosen and placed, the landscape of the dunes is elegant in the simplicity of its design. The gardeners here are fire and climate, selecting only the herbs, shrubs, and trees that can survive the rigorous constraints of this harsh environment.

Turkey oaks, some barely reaching ten feet tall, can be more than a century old. Like gnarled fingers their roots grasp for each mineral and drop of water they can eek from the dry, nutrient-poor sands. Single longleaf pines tower above the diminutive oaks and hardy shrubs. Small mats of needles and leaves are scattered like throw rugs along the hallways of sand that are regularly swept clean by wind and flames.

Rains come, but sift quickly through the sand, emerging at the base of the dunes as seeps. Most plants stand alone or in small enclaves, encircled by patches of brittle lichens and mosses that become soft and spongy when wet. The air is sweetly scented like a vintage perfume and the lungs are pleased to breathe deeply of the soothing vapors of rosemary, pine, and rare woody-stemmed mints.

Shells, bones, tracks, and burrows bear witness to a vast community of animals that find sanctuary in this sandhill habitat, including the gopher tortoise, eastern indigo snake, and the Ohoopee Narraga, a rare moth found only here. Though the dune system stretches more than thirty miles and covers close to forty thousand acres along the eastern sides of the Ohoopee and Canoochee river systems, only several hundred acres of this precious environment are protected.

Do not be deceived by its vastness. This coastal plain frontier is under great pressure from conversion to pine plantations, random home development, and fire suppression — all of which threaten to permanently alter this fragile environment. The modern age is pressing in. Yet there is still so much to be discovered here.

Stand on the sand
of the Ohoopee Dunes,
and see in all directions.

Look to the east, to the rising sun.
Give thanks for your ancestors
and all that is past.

Look to the south, to the warmth and the light.
See what you love and what you long for.
Give thanks for length of days,
for abundance and blessings.

Look to the west, to the setting sun,
the home of thunder,
the great unknown,
and the power of change.
Give thanks for your future
and the things you cannot foresee.

Look to the north, the home of winter.
Give thanks for stark truth,
for wisdom, and for the limitations
that construct the challenges of our work.

Return to the east, to the rising sun.
Stand in the center of your life.
Look to the sky
for fresh ideas and inspiration,
to the earth below for grounding,
and start your day renewed.

When you walk this circle
of the medicine wheel,
your life will be a prayer.

Bleached bones
lie in place
where a raccoon took
its last breath,
completing
a perfect circle of life
and death.

MARITIME STRAND FORESTS

Along the Georgia Coast, where saltwater rivers ebb and flow, the maritime strand forests rise up from the marshes like ghost ships against a wide, flat horizon. Some loom large with dark interiors, guarding the edges of the mainland and the marsh borders of barrier islands. Others are small, peculiar landmarks, just a few acres in size.

Heat waves shimmer over these strands built upon marsh mud, shell middens, and shifting sands, conjuring up visions of pirates and the lure of buried treasure. Like castaways we venture along the edge of a narrow strand, stepping over broken rafts of dried marsh grass and driftwood that washed up with the wreckage of the last high tide. Live oak and red cedar lean out in strange shapes; their long arms extend a wary welcome.

Cautiously we step into the interior, thankful for the green shade that provides shelter from a blazing summer sun. Trying in vain to walk with stealth, we announce our presence with the crashing sound of brittle palmetto fronds and oyster shells crunching underfoot. Yaupon holly and wax myrtle form a thick understory, and cabbage palms rattle ominously in the constant breeze. The sandy ground is camouflaged with the small leaves of live oak in muted colors of olive, soft gold, and brown. Bleached bones lie in place where a raccoon took its last breath, completing a perfect circle of life and death.

Though they look deserted from the sea, these strands, commonly known as hammocks, are life rafts of high ground. Migrating songbirds find much-needed food and rest, and wading birds, such as herons, egrets, and endangered woodstorks, roost and nest here. Whether large or small, the hammocks are home to a wide variety of species of plants and animals.

As wild places become fewer and fewer, these maritime strands serve as last refuges for coastal wildlife and protect the mainland from the forces of winds, tides, and storms. Still, pressures are mounting to reach and develop them, to gain access by building roads, bridges, and causeways.

From the edge of the strand, we look to the west as the sun sets over a last lonely stretch of saltmarsh. The exotic scent of cedar is strong here, as if trying to preserve the treasure of the hammocks — last outposts in a developing coastland.

The hammocks
stand on shifting sand,
pencil-sketched
against the horizon,

taking the wind and floods
in the midst of the saltmarsh,

guarding with live oak,
preserving with cedar,
embracing their
lonely treasures.

Look to the hammocks
as refuge —
as does the woodstork
with wings outstretched —

and what is endangered within you
will at last find sanctuary.

The hickories here

give meaning

to the words

height

and stature;

to lean against one

is to know

strength.

UPLAND MARITIME FOREST

When explorers first discovered the upland maritime forests on barrier islands and at the edges of Georgia's coastal rivers, they must have felt like they were walking in a dream. It is a land of shadows and shafts of light, vines and Spanish moss waving in the breeze, and resurrection fern cascading from bending boughs of live oak trees.

It takes time to get to know this place. One wants to look up, down, and all around at once. The groundcover is lush with grasses and ferns and thick with patches of saw palmetto. There is a sweet smell of split cedar, of earth, and of leaves. In the understory, perfectly postured magnolias and hollies wear their smooth bark in mottled shades of grey-green lichens; their glossy leaves shine.

The hickories here give meaning to the words height and stature; to lean against one is to know strength, for trees of such great girth are long gone in most places. The ground is littered with leaves, gnawed hickory nuts, and faded oyster shells from bygone days. Vines climb high into the treetops, and their aerial roots wave like tack in a steady sea-breeze.

It is quiet today — no sound save the soft tap of a woodpecker and the swishing of the wind through the oak leaves. Well-rooted in the sandy soil, laurel oaks and live oaks create a canopy with branches shaped by the wind. Though many lean and some have fallen, the trees seem to work together, sharing support and giving their mass to enrich the life of the woods. Through the years, this eco-system has given food and shelter to wildlife and to this day it provides a resting place for songbirds on long journeys.

Spared from plantation, plow, and ax, this upland maritime forest we visit is preserved as a park. It is a jewel, but just a small remnant of its original grandeur. Others like it are quickly disappearing as pressure to build home sites invades this habitat at the edges of marshes and tidal rivers.

Through the windows of the dark forest, the golden light of sunset settles on the marsh as the tide turns the river. The scent of salt is in the air, and the driftwood of downed cedars separates the woods from the bright water's edge.

These grand forests have watched over us for centuries, protected us from storms, and given sustenance to many. Now it is time, for the sake of the life within them, and for our own sake, to take notice and guard them before they disappear.

I am hardwood and evergreen,
a forest by the sea.

I stand through the storm
and the tide.

On the middens
I find my form,

where the people
drank the oyster's sweet juice.

I miss the people —
how they stopped to listen to the wind,

danced sacred dances,
sang sacred songs.

I loved their laughter,
their stories,
and the sounds of children playing.

For I, too, am a family,
rising and falling —
laurel oaks leaning upon the hickories —
leaving space for the up and coming.

I am of the old ones.
And when you come to see me,

I feel young again.

The spirit soars
with a sense of adventure,
and the imagination
is free to explore
like a child
in a land
of a thousand
fairy tales.

LONGLEAF PINE UPLAND FOREST (LONGLEAF PINE - WIREGRASS)

The longleaf pine-wiregrass community once graced more than ninety million acres of the southeastern United States. Land use over the past two centuries cut this tapestry into a patchwork of remnants now covering less than three percent of its original territory.

We travel to southwest Georgia on a cool October morning to see one of the best examples of old-growth longleaf pine forest that remains. We arrive just in time to see its lush groundcover in peak bloom. Like commoners about to be knighted, we stand weak-kneed as we enter this kingdom, spellbound by its abundance and pristine beauty.

Towering pines topped in shimmering green lean in quiet confidence, as if planning how to protect the life of their precious keep. The ground is covered in a carpet of native wildflowers, woven in threads of purple, red, and gold. Waves of wiregrass roll over the hills and sharp spikes of palmetto peek from among the ferns.

Vistas are open and park-like as the underbrush is periodically cleared by fire, which is fueled and carried by the wiregrass. One can see so far as if to be looking back in time. The spirit soars with a sense of adventure here and the imagination is free to explore like a child in a land of a thousand fairy tales.

In this forest, trees of all ages grow together. Young pines wait to be initiated by flames before filling the spaces between trees that have seen centuries. Scars from lightning — the original source of fire in this community — linger on blackened trunks.

More than two hundred rare species of plants and animals maintain a precarious hold in these remnant forests, including the endangered hummingbird flower, gopher tortoise, and red-cockaded woodpecker. The diversity here rivals that of the rainforest — in some cases fifty different species of plants in a square meter.

Centuries of forest conversion, fragmentation, and fire suppression have severed vital threads that hold this habitat together. Now, human intervention is needed to restore and maintain the health of these natural communities.

Though the longleaf pine forests offer us long sight, we cannot see the future. But as the warmth of the rising sun draws the mist from this lush land, it awakens within us a sense of hope for this forest's return.

The land remembers
the time
before time —

a place
that we catch glimpses of

in a flash of wing or pine.

It feels no need to hold on
like we do.

For the Earth
is that strange stardust,
through and through.

What strength it has
not to shout
or cry out
what it knows about

But only whispers and hints,
honors our choice to stand alone,

and welcomes us
when we want to come home.

113

KEY FEATURES, STEWARDSHIP, AND CONSERVATION STATUS OF SITES

These sketches provide background information about the sites chosen to represent the twenty-five natural communities featured in this volume. Comments on species of conservation concern and threats to the environment were provided by Dr. Jonathan Ambrose of the Wildlife Resources Division, Georgia Department of Natural Resources.

Most of these photographs were taken at locations that host the best remaining examples of this habitat type in Georgia. The sites may contain rare or endangered plant and animal species and are highly vulnerable to any kind of disturbance. Please contact the land steward for information about access and use the utmost care and respect when visiting.

We encourage you to support and get involved with the stewardship agencies and organizations listed here, along with other state and local conservation organizations, to find out how you can help in the protection and restoration of Georgia's native environments.

I

Mountain and Piedmont Springs

Location of Photograph: Blue Hole Spring, Crockford-Pigeon Mountain Wildlife Management Area

County: Walker

Time of Year: November

Stewardship: Georgia Department of Natural Resources

Access: Open to the Public

Key Features: Blue color of water, constant fifty-six-degree temperature, hydrological discharge of the Ellison Cave system.

Comments: Species of conservation concern include coldwater darter and Tennessee yellow-eyed grass. Threats include recreational overuse of springs, sedimentation from adjacent land disturbance, damming of outflows or capping and pumping of springs for water supplies, and groundwater contamination. Springs with high water-quality and intact surrounding vegetation are uncommon.

5

Mountain River

Location of Photograph: Chattooga River, Chattahoochee National Forest

County: Rabun

Time of Year: November

Stewardship: United States Forest Service

Access: Open to the Public

Key Feature: Designated Wild and Scenic River, protected streamside corridors of hemlock with evergreen heaths of rosebay rhododendron and mountain laurel; cold, highly oxygenated water, scenic gorges, native brook trout.

Comments: Species of conservation concern include the hellbender (a giant salamander), sicklefin redhorse (a fish), and *Virginia spirea*. Threats include dams, sedimentation, point source pollution, non-native invasive species and loss or removal of streamside vegetation. This is a fairly common environment in the Blue Ridge, with some excellent examples found on public land (e.g., Chattahoochee National Forest). High quality examples in the Cumberland Plateau and Ridge and Valley are less common.

8

Blackwater Branch or Creek Swamp

Location of Photograph: Yuchi Wildlife Management Area

County: Burke

Time of Year: April

Stewardship: Georgia Department of Natural Resources

Access: Open to the public

Key Features: Clear tannin-stained water, white-sand stream beds, cypress and tupelo trees, seasonal inundation, narrow flood plain.

Comments: Species of conservation concern include bluenose shiner and lax water-milfoil. Threats include physical disturbance to headwaters or streambanks, dams, point and non-point source pollution. This is a common habitat type in the Coastal Plain, but one that is impacted by a wide variety of human activities.

10

Alluvial River and Swamp System – Coastal Plain

Location of Photograph: Moody Forest Natural Area

County: Appling

Time of Year: July

Stewardship: The Nature Conservancy and Georgia Department of Natural Resources

Access: Contact The Nature Conservancy or Georgia Department of Natural Resources

Key Features: Old growth trees, some in excess of six hundred years of age, massive tupelo and bald cypress trees, seasonal flood marks on trees more than twelve feet above the ground.

Comments: Species of conservation concern include robust redhorse, greenfly orchid, Altamaha spinymussel, and Mississippi kites. Threats include non-native invasive species (e.g. feral hogs, flathead catfish, Chinese privet), non-point source pollution, upstream dams, forest conversion, and excessive sedimentation. This is a large-scale habitat type that covers much of the Coastal Plain, but which has been impacted significantly by effects of upstream dams.

12

Tidewater River and Swamp System

Location of Photograph: Buffalo Swamp

County: McIntosh

Time of Year: July

Stewardship: Georgia Department of Natural Resources

Access: Roadside view

Key Feature: Freshwater river under tidal influence, tupelo and cypress trees, broad floodplains, abundant wildlife.

Comments: Species of conservation concern include tidal marsh obedient plant, swallow-tailed kite, and shortnose sturgeon. Restricted to freshwater tidal zones of the coast. Although this habitat is less impacted than many other aquatic systems because of its topographic setting, it is still threatened by point and non-point source pollution and habitat fragmentation.

30

Bog Swamp

Location of Photograph: Chesser Prairie, Okefenokee National Wildlife Refuge

County: Ware

Time of Year: December

Stewardship: U.S. Fish and Wildlife Service

Access: Stephen C. Foster State Park and Okefenokee Swamp Park

Key Features: Vast, open wetland with floating islands of peat — called batteries — in varying stages of succession, wintering grounds for sandhill cranes.

Comments: Species of concern include sandhill crane, round-tailed muskrat, parrot pitcherplant. The Okefenokee Swamp is a unique wetland system, a complex of several different wetland communities. Threats include hydrologic alterations, fire suppression, disturbance of upland buffer areas, and potential disturbance from mining to exploit mineral resources.

31

Cypress Savannah

Location of Photograph: Big Duke's Pond Natural Area
County: Jenkins
Time of Year: August
Stewardship: Georgia Department of Natural Resources
Access: Contact Georgia Department of Natural Resources
Key Features: Massive pond cypress, nesting site for woodstorks, minimal shrub layer
Comments: Species of concern include Canby's dropwort and flatwoods salamander. High quality examples of this wetland type are rare. Threats include fire suppression, hydrologic alterations (primarily ditching), and conversion to agricultural or silvicultural uses.

32

Herb Bog

Location of Photograph: Doerun Pitcherplant Bog Natural Area
County: Colquitt
Time of Year: April
Stewardship: Georgia Department of Natural Resources
Access: Open to the public
Key Features: Nestled in a low-lying area within a longleaf pine forest. A variety carnivorous plants including parrot pitcherplant, trumpet pitcherplant, and sundew.
Comments: Species of concern include purple honeycomb-head, chaffseed, and spotted turtle. Formerly much more widespread in the Coastal Plain; today, extensive, intact examples are rare. Threats include fire suppression or burning in wrong season, ditching, grazing, plant collecting, and forest conversion.

34

Mountain and Piedmont Bog; Spring Seep

Location of Photograph: Chattahoochee National Forest
County: Rabun
Time of Year: August
Stewardship: United States Forest Service
Access: Access restricted due to rarity of habitat and on-going restoration work.
Key Features: One of the last remaining mountain bogs in Georgia. Mountaintop location, shallow flowing water, abundant sphagnum moss, surrounded by mountain laurel, habitat of purple pitcherplant and bog turtle.
Comments: Species of concern include purple pitcherplant and bog turtle (mountain), and monkeyface orchid (piedmont). Mountain bogs are rare habitats. Piedmont bogs are very rare and intact examples at low elevations are essentially unknown, probably wiped out by land use changes years ago. Threats include hydrologic alterations, livestock grazing, plant collecting, fire suppression, and in some cases, exclusion or removal of beaver.

Sagpond

Location of Photograph: Crockford-Pigeon Mountain Wildlife Management Area

County: Walker

Time of Year: September

Stewardship: Georgia Department of Natural Resources

Access: Open to the public

Key Features: Moist or water-filled depressions found where underlying limestone is dissolved by groundwater, a wide variety of habitat types ranging from open water to forested wetland. Plants includes rare sedges and grasses, and wide-based black gum trees.

Comments: Species of concern include tussock sedge and featherfoil; the fauna is poorly known—mole salamander (not rare) is a typical species. An uncommon habitat type; intact examples are rare. Threats include ditching and draining, conversion of vegetated buffer zones to agricultural or silvicultural uses, and residential development. Only a few examples are under any form of protection.

Bluff and Ravine Forest

Location of Photograph: Blacks Bluff Preserve

County: Floyd

Time of Year: March

Stewardship: The Nature Conservancy

Access: Contact The Nature Conservancy

Key Features: Scenic, steep, north-facing bluffs, diverse plant communities with plants of northern affinity.

Comments: A fairly common habitat type, but impacted by residential development, road construction, non-native invasive plant species, and forest conversion. Species of concern include limerock arrowwood, three-flower hawthorn, and seepage salamander (in wet areas).

Ravine, Gorge, and Cove Forest

Location of Photograph: Cloudland Canyon State Park

County: Dade

Time of Year: November

Stewardship: Georgia Department of Natural Resources

Access: Open to the Public

Key Features of Cloudland Canyon: Cloudland Canyon is a superb example this environment type. Nearly perpendicular sandstone cliffs, forested talus slopes, scenic waterfalls. Virginia and shortleaf pine, black birch, and hemlock near the streams.

Comments: A fairly common habitat type, but intact, protected examples are uncommon. Species of concern include green salamander (in moist rock crevices) and goldenseal. Threats include residential development, road construction, forest conversion, and loss of scenic value through inappropriate development.

47

Armuchee Ridge Forest

Location of Photograph: Marshall Forest Preserve

County: Floyd

Time of Year: March

Stewardship: The Nature Conservancy

Access: Contact The Nature Conservancy

Key Features: Mixed pine-hardwood forest communities of great diversity, steep, narrow ridges, and unusual combination of northern and southern tree species.

Comments: Fairly widespread and variable in composition within relatively small geographic area of Ridge and Valley. Species of concern include northern pine snake and pink ladyslipper. Threats include fragmentation, altered fire regime, forest conversion, and road/utility/residential development.

48

Cedar Glades

Location of Photograph: Chickamauga and Chattanooga National Military Park

County: Catoosa

Time of Year: April

Stewardship: National Park Service

Access: Open to the Public

Key Features: Open and park-like environment with thin rocky soil, groundcover of grasses and herbs. Eastern red cedar is the dominant tree, high diversity of plant species.

Comments: Rare habitat type in Georgia; most examples are in Chickamauga-Chattanooga National Military Park. Species of concern include least gladecress and Great Plains ladies-tresses. Threats include fire suppression, non-native invasive species, and road development.

Coosa Valley Prairies – Wet Prairie

Location of Photograph: Coosa Valley Prairie

County: Floyd

Time of Year: August

Stewardship: Temple-Inland Forest and The Nature Conservancy

Access: Contact The Nature Conservancy. The Georgia Botanical Society occasionally leads field trips here.

Key Features: Open prairie-like environment, dominated by grass and forbs, wet clayey soils, high diversity of plant species, including prairie dock and the rare whorled sunflower.

Comments: Very rare habitat confined to Ridge and Valley. Species of concern include whorled sunflower and Coosa Barbara's-buttons. Threats include conversion to silvicultural use, hydrologic alteration, non-native invasive species, and fire suppression.

49b

Coosa Valley Prairies – Dry Prairie

Location of Photograph: Coosa Valley Prairies
County: Floyd
Time of Year: May
Stewardship: Temple Inland Forest and The Nature Conservancy
Access: Contact The Nature Conservancy. The Georgia Botanical Society occasionally leads field trips here.
Key Features: Open, prairie-like environment, heavy clay soils, prairie purple coneflower, prairie dock.
Comments: Very rare habitat confined to Ridge & Valley. Species of concern include Bachman's sparrow and prairie purple coneflower. Threats include conversion to silvicultural use, residential development, non-native invasive species, and fire suppression.

50

Rock Outcrops – Cumberland Plateau

Location of Photograph: Rocktown, Crockford-Pigeon Mountain Wildlife Management Area
County: Walker
Time of Year: November
Stewardship: Georgia Department of Natural Resources
Access: Open to the Public
Key Features: Towering sandstone rock formations, iron ore and marine fossils in the rocks, a combination of dry- and moisture-loving plants.
Comments: Not rare, but restricted primarily to rim of Lookout, Sand, and Pigeon Mountain. Species of concern include showy tickseed and eastern woodrat. Threats include residential development, recreational overuse, and possibly fire suppression.

53

Boulderfields

Location of Photograph: Sosebee Cove, Chattahoochee National Forest
County: Lumpkin
Time of Year: May
Stewardship: United States Forest Service
Access: Open to the public
Key Features: A very lush environment, large angular boulders covered in mosses, plant and animal species of northern affinity.
Comments: Rare habitat type, naturally restricted by topographic setting (slope, elevation, aspect), seldom found below altitudes of 3,200 feet. Some very good examples are found on public land (Chattachoochee National Forest). Species of concern include rock shrew and mountain maple. Most known examples are protected; however global warming, non-native invasive species, and road/utility construction remain as threats.

54

Oak Ridge Forest

Location of Photograph: Black Rock Mountain State Park
County: Rabun
Time of Year: April
Stewardship: Georgia Department of Natural Resources
Access: Open to the Public
Key Features: Found on upper slopes and ridges, stunted trees with twisted and gnarled branches shaped by weather, evergreen heath understory.
Comments: Fairly common forest type in the Blue Ridge; a few old-growth examples are known. Species of concern include ash-leaved bush-pea and masked shrew. Threats include residential/road/utility development and forest conversion.

68

Oak-Hickory Climax Forest

Location of Photograph: Georgia Forestry Commission, Dawsonville Office
County: Dawson
Time of Year: April
Stewardship: Georgia Forestry Commission
Access: Contact Georgia Forestry Commission
Key Features: Mature forest dominated by oaks and hickories. Open woods with a well developed sub-canopy and a sparse ground cover of spring-blooming wildflowers.
Comments: Once a predominant habitat of the Piedmont, now relatively rare and confined to areas that were not suitable for agriculture. Most "recovering" examples have disturbed understory/groundlayer vegetation. Special concern species include yellow ladyslipper, Georgia aster, and loggerhead shrike (in open woods). Threats include development of all kinds, fire suppression, forest conversion, and non-native invasive species.

76

Rock Outcrops – Piedmont

Location of Photograph: Heggie's Rock Preserve
County: Columbia
Time of Year: April
Stewardship: The Nature Conservancy
Access: Contact The Nature Conservancy
Key Features: Exposed granite covered in patches of lichens and mosses, colorful dish gardens, many rare and endemic plants, excellent example of primary plant succession.
Comments: Granite outcrops in the Georgia Piedmont are uncommon, small-patch habitats, and pristine examples are rare. Species of concern include poolsprite, black-spored quillwort, and Stone Mountain fairy shrimp. Threats include quarrying, trash dumping, sedimentation, non-native invasive species, recreational overuse, and vandalism.

86

Dwarf Oak - Evergreen Shrub Forest

Location of Photograph: Ohoopee Dunes Natural Area

County: Emmanuel

Time of Year: November

Stewardship: Georgia Department of Natural Resources

Access: Open to the public

Key Features: Found primarily on deep, coarse-sand dunes along the Ohoopee and Canoochee river systems. Open, desert-like appearance, a variety of aromatic herbs and shrubs, stunted turkey oaks, isolated longleaf pines, and gopher tortoise habitat.

Comments: Restricted to areas with deep sand, these are rare habitats in Georgia. Species of concern include sandhills rosemary and indigo snake. Threats include fire suppression, conversion to silvicultural or agricultural uses, residential development, and sand mining.

88

Maritime Strand Forest

Location of Photograph: Ossabaw Island Heritage Preserve

County: Chatham

Time of Year: July

Stewardship: Georgia Department of Natural Resources

Access: Contact the Ossabaw Island Foundation or Georgia Department of Natural Resources

Key Features: Many appear as small islands in a sea of salt marsh. Commonly known as marsh hammocks. Live oak, red cedar, and cabbage palm, important feeding and nesting grounds for wading birds, refuge for marsh carnivores such as mink and raccoon.

Comments: Restricted to low marsh islands and marsh borders of barrier islands, these are rare habitats. Threats include residential and road development, recreational overuse, and non-native plant and animal invasive species. Species of concern include Godfrey's wild privet and diamondback terrapin.

89

Upland Maritime Forest

Location of Photograph: Crooked River State Park

County: Camden

Time of Year: December

Stewardship: Georgia Department of Natural Resources

Access: Open to the public

Key Features: Jungle-like in appearance. A mature forest of broadleaf evergreens including live oak, laurel oak, American holly, and southern magnolia intermixed with red bay, hickories, cabbage palm, and slash pine with tropical vegetation. Provides shade, wildlife habitat, and aids in prevention of rapid runoff of rains.

Comments: An uncommon habitat; Georgia has most of the protected maritime forest on the Atlantic coast. Remaining unprotected sites are threatened by development of all kinds, non-native invasive plant and animal species and fire suppression. Species of concern include painted bunting and climbing buckthorn.

Longleaf Pine Upland Forest (Longleaf Pine - Wiregrass)

Location of Photograph: The Big Woods, Greenwood Plantation

County: Thomas County

Time of Year: October

Stewardship: The Greentree Foundation. At the time the photograph was taken, in October of 2003, the site was being managed by The Nature Conservancy. TNC no longer manages this site.

Access: Contact The Greentree Foundation

Key Features: Best example of longleaf pine-wiregrass community in the region. Two-to-four-hundred-year-old longleaf pines, open woodland with lush groundcover including wiregrass and a great variety of wildflower species.

Comments: Once the predominant habitat type of Coastal Plain uplands, this habitat is now rare throughout its former range. Species of concern include red-cockaded woodpecker, gopher tortoise, Catesby's bindweed, and wire-leaf dropseed. Threats include altered fire regime, residential/commercial development, non-native invasive species (e.g., cogon grass), and forest conversion.

ANN FOSKEY

From counting sea turtle hatchlings on Sapelo Island to organizing statewide heritage education conferences, Ann Foskey has dedicated her professional career to creating and implementing programs that foster awareness of the need to protect our state's natural and cultural resources. She has a Master's degree in Heritage Preservation from Georgia State University and a Bachelor of Science degree in Natural Science with Environmental Emphasis from Shorter College in Rome, Georgia.

Ann has worked as a naturalist, researcher, and writer for the Georgia Department of Natural Resources, a conference coordinator for the Georgia Trust for Historic Preservation, and as an Associate Archeologist for the Georgia Power Company. In 2001, she published her first book, *Ossabaw Island*, a pictorial history of Georgia's third largest barrier island, and since then has been working as freelance writer.

"My parents must have known that I was destined to become a writer when, at the age of four, I etched the alphabet into the soft wood of my bedroom window sill. I have always loved letters. They are elegant and architectural, the building blocks of my craft.

They must have suspected I would become a naturalist when they saw how I cherished the things of the earth — the soft, white fur of the pussy willow, a salamander's tiny hands, and the gold and silver stones I found by the brook near our house. To this day, I have yet to find anything that captivates me more than the mysteries of the natural world.

There is a silent voice that calls to me through nature. All my life I have heard it and pursued it. I even tried to discover what it is through studying the laws of science. But the more I chased it, the farther away it seemed to be.

Only recently have I come to realize that the way for me to find out what is calling from behind the veil of nature is to enter into it and create with it. When I apply myself to nature, using my thoughts, impressions, and skills in the craft of writing, things slowly begin to take shape. I am beginning to discover, through my poetry and prose, some of the forces behind what I perceive. My job is to pay attention and respond. And as a reward for my efforts, nature reveals some of her secrets to me."

MARC DEL SANTRO

Marc Del Santro specializes in wildlife and nature photography, in which he combines his photographic skills with his passion for the outdoors — creating thought provoking and emotionally stirring images with the hope of increasing people's awareness of and concern for the environment. Marc's work is a regular feature in Georgia Backroads magazine and selected pieces have been accessioned into the permanent collection of the Fernbank Museum of Natural History in Atlanta, Georgia.

His love of nature began at an early age, growing up in northeastern Pennsylvania, where through many adventures, mishaps, and hard lessons, he learned to respect nature, to tread lightly, and to leave nothing behind. He also learned to be still, to sit quietly, and to watch and listen. Through this Marc began to appreciate the subtle and unexpected treasures nature always provides for us, and to take in more deeply what he saw.

"As I grew older I began to realize that I was receiving my greatest lesson of all — to move with nature, to listen closely, and to follow her lead."

Marc's strong intrepid nature and desire to escape his city surroundings led him to explore farther and farther into the wilderness, and also helped him better understand his deep spiritual connection with nature and all things wild. This connection is evident in his writing and his photography.

Marc's interest in photography was sparked at the age of twelve when he found his father's camera from his days as a soldier.

"It was a mechanical camera, an old rangefinder. I had never seen anything like it before. I spent many days investigating the workings of every button, dial, and lever until I figured out what everything did and how it all tied together.

It wasn't long before I set off on my first photographic expedition — my destination, a partially frozen lake where a pair of ducks had chosen to winter over. I slowly walked out onto the ice and started taking

pictures of the wary ducks. Although I was aware of the potential for danger, I felt somehow protected. I also felt the risk I was taking was worth the adventure and decided to carry on. For better or for worse, this is a character trait that I possess to this day.

When I saw the developed prints from that day, something awakened inside me. I realized I had a means to bring home with me and to share with others the incredible magic of what I saw and felt when I was out in the wild. It was at this point my interest in photography turned into a passion."

Throughout his professional career, Marc Del Santro also has worked in corporate, fashion, advertising, industrial, and architectural photography with a client list that includes IBM, NASA, Southern Company, Georgia Power Company, Georgia Resource Center, Atlanta Regional Commission, Georgia Department of Natural Resources, and The Nature Conservancy.

ACKNOWLEDGEMENTS

We would like to thank the following individuals and organizations for their help and support in bringing Still Small Voices to life.

The late Dr. Charles H. Wharton — whose book, *The Natural Environments of Georgia*, was the inspiration for this project — for his friendship, support, and encouragement.

The late Dr. Eugene Odum — for his friendship and his fatherly advice on how to proceed with this project, and for sharing his knowledge of ecology with us over the course of a few intense lunch meetings.

Earth Share of Georgia — for serving as the non-profit umbrella for the Still Small Voices project. The organizational support of Earth Share provides a solid foundation that enables the project to live and grow.

John Beasley, President, Wakefield Beasley & Associates — John, thank you for taking us under your wing and for believing in us and our work with the Still Small Voices project. Thank you for your generosity in supporting the project and for constantly introducing it to other people, including Dan Roper of *Georgia Backroads* magazine, which led to the publication of this book. You are an amazing person and we are humbled by your graciousness. Above all, thank you, John, for being our friend.

Dan Roper, Editor and Publisher of *Georgia Backroads* magazine — Thank you, Dan for being a friend and a fan, for making Still Small Voices a part of *Georgia Backroads* magazine, and for your generosity in serving as the publisher of this book. Your integrity was evident from the first day we met. It is refreshing to work with you, as you are one of those rare breeds still willing to conduct business on a handshake. We appreciate your vision, your enthusiasm, and your lunches. Thank you, also, Darinda Stafford and Josh Owens, staff of *Georgia Backroads*, for lively conversations, friendship, and all of your hard work.

Dr. Jon Ambrose, Wildlife Resources Division, Georgia Department of Natural Resources — Thank you, Jon, for recognizing the value of Still Small Voices as a way to reach beyond the scientific community, and for being the first to provide a source of funding for this project. You continuously demonstrate unwavering faith in us and you are one of the project's greatest assets. The breadth and depth of your knowledge of natural environments and their ecology is matched by your ability to convey it in terms that most of us can understand. Thank you for your patience and your understanding of what it is that we are trying to achieve, and for all your help along the way.

Tom Patrick, Jim Allison, and Shan Cammick of the Wildlife Resources Division, Georgia Department of Natural Resources — Thank you for assisting us in locating sites, identifying plants, animals, and environments, and for helping to ensure the scientific accuracy of our work. We appreciate your patience in answering countless questions, phone calls, and emails, and for meeting us out in the field. The work you are doing to protect and restore Georgia's native environments is truly needed.

The Nature Conservancy, Georgia Chapter — Thank you to Tavia McKuen, Vice President and State Director, for all the generous help provided by The Nature Conservancy staff. Thank you Malcolm Hodges, I Ling Matthews, Todd Engstrom, Kara Land, Christine Griffiths, Christy Lambert, and Allison McGee, for providing technical expertise and facilitating access to Nature Conservancy preserves. We appreciate your help, enthusiasm, and encouragement. Your dedication to your work is an inspiration to us. It is a great pleasure to know and work with each and every one of you.

A special thanks to Malcolm Hodges for reviewing the work of the project for scientific accuracy, answering countless questions, and for helping with the logistics of finding many of these environments. Thank you, Mal.

Fernbank Museum of Natural History — Thank you to Susan Neugent, president and CEO of Fernbank Museum, for all the help of the Fernbank staff including Jennifer Grant Warner, Bill Bevil, Marie Napoli, Alison Damerow, Brandi Berry, and Christine Bean. Thank you all for recognizing the educational and inspirational value of Still Small Voices and for inviting us to exhibit at Fernbank. We appreciate the time and effort each of you gave us in promoting the Still Small Voices project. It is refreshing how easy it is to work with you.

ACKNOWLEDGEMENTS

Sam Breyfogle of Temple-Inland Forest—Thank you Sam, for the time you spent with us in the field and for providing access to the Coosa Valley Prairies. Thank you for making yourself available to us and for being sympathetic to the odd hours a nature photographer must keep.

Jim Bitler and Elizabeth DuBose of the Ossabaw Island Foundation—Thank you, Elizabeth, for allowing us access to work on Ossabaw Island, and for always being so helpful. Thank you, Jim, for your hospitality and humor, and for sharing your knowledge of the island with us, and to both of you, thank you for your friendship.

Jay Clark—Thank you, Jay, for leading us to the sagponds on Pigeon Mountain. We appreciate you taking the time to spend the day with us in the field. Good luck with your book, *Wildflowers of Pigeon Mountain*.

Chip and Joy Campbell — Thank you, Chip and Joy for your hospitality, for sharing your vast knowledge of the Okefenokee Swamp with us, and helping to make our visits to the swamp a success. Your love for and dedication to the Okefenokee is an inspiration.

For the staff of Yuchi Wildlife Management Area—Thank you for taking the time to show us around and for explaining to us the status and workings of the different natural communities found there.

Paralax Digital Imaging — David Clevenger. David, as a fellow nature photographer, thank you for taking an interest in this project. Your generosity is greatly appreciated. The superior quality of the work produced at Paralax, along with the knowledge, skill, and professionalism of your staff, is second to none.

Thomas Jones — Thank you, Tom, for your expertise in the production of the Still Small Voices images, and for your friendship all these years.

Carol and Tom Blackmon of Warehouse Framers, the best and most affordable frame shop on the planet—We always enjoy our visits to your frame shop. Thank you for your trust and your friendship and for making us feel like a part of your family.

Pisconeri Studio and Design — Judy and Tony Pishnery — Thank you, Judy and Tony, for your input on the design elements of the Still Small Voices project, answering many technical questions over the years, and for being a part of the production of the images. And thank you, also, for your unconditional friendship and continued moral support.

Full Cycle Management and Marketing, Jarrette Burkhalter and Kim Ribbans — Thank you Jarrette, for tutoring us in the art of fundraising and grant writing in the early days of the project. Thank you, Kim, for making our web site happen. And thank you both for your friendship and for donating so much of your time to help us get the Still Small Voices project started. We couldn't have done it without you.

Heather Smith — Thank you, Heather, for your generous gift of time and expertise in proofreading the first drafts of the manuscript. It meant so much to us to have you in our corner during those stressful times right before deadlines. We appreciate your talent, sensitivity, and your wonderful, ever-ready laughter. We wish you all the best.

Izora, Inc. — George Weinstein. Thank you, George, for proofing the final manuscript and also for your dedication to promoting the craft of writing through your work with the Atlanta Writer's Club.

Chris Canolis, Georgia Department of Natural Resources — Thank you, Chris for sharing your expertise in plotting the sites for the map in this book.

Jeana Aquadro — Thank you, Jeana, for walking us through the many steps we needed to take in order to prepare the work of Still Small Voices for publication. You went above and beyond and we truly appreciate your generosity of spirit. You are a fabulous teacher, a gifted designer, and your laughter radiates with the joy you have for living. It is a pleasure and a privilege to work with you. Thank you, also, to your family, John Crawford and daughter, Lauren, for their generous support during the seasons of planning, design, and production.

MARC'S PERSONAL THANKS

To my wife, Sheila

Thank you for believing in me and perhaps, more importantly, thank you for the freedom to pursue this adventure. In life and in our marriage you are everything I am not. I love you.

For Sheila and John

It must be said that our spouses, Sheila and John, are as much a part of Still Small Voices as Ann and I. It is only through both Sheila and John's remarkable patience, constant support, and never-ending encouragement that we have come this far.

On more than one occasion they have saved the day with fresh perspectives, creative suggestions, and superior computer skills. Their humor, intelligence and compassion have helped us through several frustrating incidents and even a few brief moments of self-doubt. They both have sat side by side with us through many countless hours and late nights, graciously lending their help to overcome any creative or technical problems we faced along the way.

Though Sheila and John have few opportunities to join us in the field, we recognize that theirs is the more difficult task of keeping things together at home. We truly appreciate them taking on extra responsibilities and for the sacrifices they make, which allows us to do this work. Thank you both.

To Will Foskey

Will, thank you so much for the comic relief and for providing an endless source of entertainment.

To John Reeves, a trusted friend for many years

Thank you, John, for your contribution to this project. Your fierce dedication to nature and all things wild is truly inspiring. We have had many incredible, hair-raising, awe-inspiring adventures together and we are stronger and wiser for it. Until the next adventure, my friend.

ANN'S PERSONAL THANKS

To my husband, John

Thank you for believing in me and supporting me in the things that I set out to accomplish. Without your support, this work would not have been achieved. Most especially, John, thank you for your love.

To my son, Will

Will, thank you for being so patient and understanding through the many days, nights, weeks, and months that I spent at the computer, writing. Thank you for your good advice of "doing the hardest things first" when deadlines were approaching. You are a joy to me and I am glad that you are in my life.

Thank you to Cedar Hill Enrichment Center in Gainesville for being dedicated to providing a place where people can renew their connections with Earth and Spirit, and for providing a peaceful, quiet place to work when I needed to "get-away-from-it-all" to complete the manuscript.

Thank you to my fellow writers in the Alpharetta Barnes and Noble Writer's Group and the Wednesday night Village Veranda Critique Group. Thank you for your friendship, your encouragement, and for being an inspiration to me. You are my heroes. Thank you especially, to Terri Del Campo and Kelly Bell for reading and commenting on the early versions of the poetry and prose, and to Dr. Terry Segal for sending such positive energy my way.

Thank you to my family and friends, especially my mother and father, Nancy and Bill Newman, my mother-in-law and friend, Marilyn Foskey, my sisters, Mary Hoag and Jane Newman-Jackson, and my friends, Sherilyn Jones Martin and Joan Newton. Thank you to each of you for your understanding, encouragement, prayers, patience, and unconditional love.

COLOPHON

With Still Small Voices They Speak
Published by Legacy Communications
and designed by Jeana Aquadro,
this first edition of 3,000 copies
was printed in the autumn of 2006
at Kennickell Print and Communications
in Savannah, Georgia.
The typeface is Sabon, designed by Jan Tschichold.
The paper is M-REAL Galerie Art Silk,
which is made with up to 30% recycled fiber
and with chlorine free (TCF/ECF) pulp,
produced at the Aanekoski Mill in Finland—
a totally acid free paper mill certified by Europe's
PEFC (Programme for the Endorsement of Forest Certification)—
using timber from managed forests.
The paper in this publication meets the minimum requirements
of the American National Standard for Information Sciences —
Permanence of Paper for Printed Library Materials
ANSI Z39.48-1992.
The inks are soy-based.

Marc Del Santro's photographs were shot using
Nikon cameras (two Nikon F-5 bodies) and lenses.
Lenses used were a 20 mm 2.8, a 28 mm 1.4, and a 60 mm micro.
To achieve the detail and depth of field seen in the images,
Marc used an old-school technique known as hyper-focal focusing.
The only filter used was a polarizer.
Exposures ranged from f 11 to f 22,
with shutter speeds from several seconds to several minutes.
All images were shot in 35 mm format.
Film used was Fuji Velvia 100 and Fuji Velvia 50.